RICHAI

CW00516766

A Slice of Saturday Night

A Musical

Book, music and lyrics by
The Heather Brothers

Samuel French - London
New York - Toronto - Hollywood

© 1991 BY HEATHER BROTHERS ENTERPRISES

Rights of Performance by Amateurs are controlled by Samuel French Ltd, 52 Fitzroy Street, London W1P 6JR, and they, or their authorized agents, issue licences to amateurs on payment of a fee. **It is an infringement of the Copyright to give any performance or public reading of the play before the fee has been paid and the licence issued.**

The Professional Repertory Rights in this play are controlled by SAMUEL FRENCH LTD, 52 FITZROY STREET, LONDON W1P 6JR.

The publication of this play does not imply that it is necessarily available for performance by amateurs or professionals, either in the British Isles or Overseas. Amateurs and professionals considering a production are strongly advised in their own interests to apply to appropriate agents for consent before starting rehearsals or booking a theatre or hall.

ISBN 0 573 08084 4

Please see page iv for further copyright information.

A SLICE OF SATURDAY NIGHT

First produced by the Brighton Actors Theatre at The Nightingale, Brighton and then by H.B.E. at The King's Head Theatre, London. Presented by H.B.E., The Theatre of Comedy and John P. Griffin, in association with The King's Head, at the Arts Theatre, London, on 27th September 1989, with the following cast:

Eric "Rubber Legs" de Vene	Binky Baker
Garry and Terry	David Easter
Bridget	Lisa Hollander
Sharon	Mitch Munroe
Sue	Georgia Mitchell
Rick	James Powell
Eddie	Roy Smiles
Penny and Shirl	Debi Thomson

The play directed by **Marc Urquhart**

Set design by **Gillian Daniell**
Musical Director **Keith Hayman**

The Trends:
Keith Hayman (Guitar and Keyboards)
Robert Hector (Bass)
Ian Stronach (Electric and Acoustic Guitar)

The action takes place in and around the Club A Go-Go, a "Cavern" type cellar beat club in a provincial English town

Time: the early 1960s

COPYRIGHT INFORMATION

(See also page ii)

This play is fully protected under the Copyright Laws of the British Commonwealth of Nations, the United States of America and all countries of the Berne and Universal Copyright Conventions.

All rights, including Stage, Motion Picture, Radio, Television, Public Reading, and Translation into Foreign Languages, are strictly reserved.

No part of this publication may lawfully be reproduced in ANY form or by any means—photocopying, typescript, recording (including video-recording), manuscript, electronic, mechanical, or otherwise—or be transmitted or stored in a retrieval system, without prior permission.

Licences for amateur performances are issued subject to the understanding that it shall be made clear in all advertising matter that the audience will witness an amateur performance; that the names of the authors of the plays shall be included on all announcements and on all programmes; and that the integrity of the authors' work will be preserved.

The Royalty Fee is subject to contract and subject to variation at the sole discretion of Samuel French Ltd.

In Territories Overseas the fee quoted in this Acting Edition may not apply. A fee will be quoted on application to our local authorized agent, or if there is no such agent, on application to Samuel French Ltd, London.

VIDEO RECORDING OF AMATEUR PRODUCTIONS

Please note that the copyright laws governing video-recording are extremely complex and that it should not be assumed that any play may be video-recorded *for whatever purpose* without first obtaining the permission of the appropriate agents. The fact that a play is published by Samuel French Ltd does not indicate that video rights are available or that Samuel French Ltd controls such rights.

MUSICAL NUMBERS

Prologue

A Slice of Saturday Night

Act I

Club A Go-Go
Waiting
Saturday Night Chat
Seventeen
Don't Touch Me
Twiggy
Cliff
Love On Our Side
What Do I Do Now?
What Do You Do?
If You Wanna Have Fun
The Long Walk Back
Romance/Wham Bam
The Boy Of My Dreams
It Wouldn't Be Saturday Night Without a Fight

Act II

Eric's Hokey-Cokey Shuffle
I Fancy You
Sentimental Eyes
Heartbreaker
Eric's Gonna Keep Going
Oh So Bad
Please Don't Tell Me
You're Oh, So ...
Lies
Baby I Love You
P.E.
Who'd Be Seventeen
Last Saturday Night
A Slice of Saturday Night/Club A Go-Go (reprise)

PROLOGUE

The Lights pick out seven teenagers in various stages of dress getting ready for Saturday night. They are:

Gary, a good looking, hunky, chauvinistic braggart. Think's he is God's gift to women. The leader of the gang of boys. Acts tough but when it comes to it is a bit of a coward

Rick, the innocent of the group, shy, but very engaging. He looks up to Gary and tries to imitate him

Eddie, a real pill-popping goon-ball. He appears stupid, but there is more to him than meets the eye

Bridget, (Frigid Bridget as she is known to the boys), is the natural leader of the girls. She considers herself a cut above everyone else in the Club. A rather imposing girl

Sue is Gary's long-suffering girl friend. She adores Gary. She is slightly over weight with a big bust; is totally insecure and has rather a low opinion of herself. She is constantly putting on a brave face and holding back the tears

Sharon, the new girl. Rick's female equivalent. Sweet and shy, a pretty girl in an ordinary "girl next door" way

Penny, is the "easy" girl of the club. Much sexier and more knowing than the others. Attractive in a brassy way

They face the audience, as though looking into a mirror as they put on make-up and get dressed. Their hair styles and clothes epitomize the period. By the end of the song they are ready

Song: A Slice of Saturday Night

All   Gonna take me a slice of Saturday night.
                 Gonna take me a slice of Saturday night.
                 Gonna take me a slice of Saturday night, tonight,
                     tonight.
                 Gonna take me a slice of Saturday night.
                 Saturday night
                 Gonna take me, take me a slice
                 Of Saturday night.
                 Saturday night.
                 Saturday night.
                 Saturday night.

Bridget   Got my mini skirt.

Eddie	Got my knitted tie.
Sue	Got my false eye lashes.
Penny	Got my fishnet tights.
Rick	Got my hipster trousers.
Sharon	Got my pink lipstick.
Gary	Got my Chelsea boots on.
	Man, I really look hip.

All I'm so cool,
Real trendy.
So fab,
So . . . yeah, yeah, yeah!
Saturday night.

Penny	Meet some fellas
All	Saturday night.
Rick	Grab me some chicks.
All	Saturday night.
Sue	Dig the music.
All	Saturday night.
Eddie	Drink till I'm sick.
All	Saturday night.
Sharon	Dance like crazy.
All	Saturday night.
Bridget	Hear all the chat.
All	Saturday night.
Gary	Have a good time,
	Man, cos that's where it's at.

All I'm so cool.
Real Trendy.
So fab.
So . . . yeah, yeah, yeah, yeah!
Gonna take me a slice of Saturday night.
Gonna take me a slice of Saturday night.
Gonna take me a slice of Saturday night, tonight,
     tonight.
Gonna take me a slice of Saturday night.
Saturday night.
Gonna take me, take me a slice
Of Saturday night.

Voice (*off; speaking angrily*) Are you still in that bleeding bathroom?

All   Saturday night!

They reach up and switch off the Lights

Black-out

ACT I

The Club A Go-Go

The composite setting comprises the entrance to the Club, the Club itself, outside the Club and the Ladies' and Gents' toilets, as well as providing space for the Band

The Lights pick out Eric "Rubber Legs" de Vene, a forty-year-old rocker, dressed in black dinner jacket, dress shirt and bow tie, who is standing at the entrance of the Club. Eric owns the Club. A hard man with a soft spot for his patrons

Song: Club A Go-Go

Eric   (*to audience*) The name is Eric "Rubber Legs" de Vene.

(*speaking*) Hello ... I said, "Hello"! ... Right!
>Niceties over, I'll set the scene.
>The time's around nineteen sixty-four.
>A year either way but it could be more.
>When the hems were high and the fringes low,
>And Saturday night meant the Club A Go-Go.

The Lights come up to reveal the Club. The purple walls are covered with posters and coloured festoons.

> *Gary and Sue enter with Sharon, a new girl, who gazes round at the Club*

Gary pays Eric and he stamps their hands. Gary crosses and talks to the Band. Sue and Sharon sit down on chairs 1 and 2

>Though it all takes place in this club of mine.
>It could be any from around that time.
>Though they may have had a diff'rent name,

Sue crosses and asks Gary to dance. He tells her he is talking to the Band. She sits down again on chair two

>The kids you'd find inside were all the same.
>With the music loud and the lights down low
>Any club could've been the Club A Go-Go.

Sue again crosses and asks Gary to dance. An argument breaks out

>The kids don't come here just to dance.
>The club is where they get their first taste of Romance.
>Couples meet and couples drift apart.

Gary storms off R *to the bar*

But Eric's always here to mend a broken heart.

Sue sits down next to Sharon

Penny enters and pays Eric

They treat the club like a home from home,

Eric gooses Penny

And I treat them as though they were my own.

Penny joins the girls on chair three

(*Shouting angrily at someone in the audience*) 'Ere, if I catch you writing on the walls once more, I'll break your bleeding fingers . . . Kapiche!

(*Singing*) So I'd like to welcome you one and all.
To one of life's great finishing schools.
The breeding ground of the teenage dream.
A microcosm of the teenage scene.
Where the kids learnt all they had to know,
On Saturday night at the Club A Go-Go.

Eddie enters with a large overcoat slung over his shoulder, which is obviously concealing someone else

Eddie pays Eric for one. As he starts to cross Eric pulls off the coat to reveal a sheepish Rick, crouching beneath. The girls laugh at Rick

(*Speaking*) I know you're a bit of an arse-hole, Rick, but let's not get carried away . . . Out!
Rick But, Eric . . .
Eric Out! (*To Eddie*) And you . . . Don't try it on, all right?

Eddie exits R *to the bar*

Rick exits to the street

(*Singing*) Where the music's loud and the lights are
    low,
And Saturday night,
Ev'ry Saturday night
Meant the Club A Go-Go.

Bridget enters, pays and crosses to the other girls

Saturday night at the Club A Go-Go!

The girls all move up a chair so Bridget can sit down. Eric pours himself a drink and sits at his desk. The girls chat

Song: Waiting

Girls   We arrive at the Club
                                   Ev'ry Saturday night.

> Having spent hours grooming,
> Plucking and pruning,
> To get our hair and our make-up just right.
> We've scanned through the pages
> Of *Fab* magazine,
> Making sure our gear's still
> "In", in the "in-in scene".
> Still in, in the "in scene",
> As seen in *Fab* magazine.
> We arrive and at once
> Disappear in the loo.

The girls follow Bridget into the loo

> For the ritual check-up,
> Hair, gear and make-up,
> As girls always tradition'lly do.
> The "once over", over,
> Checked from head to toe,
> A day's preparation's
> About to go on show.
> We burst on to the scene,

The girls follow Bridget back into the Club and take up model poses

> Straight out of *Fab* magazine.

Gary and Eddie enter from the bar and cross to chat with Eric

The girls sit down

> After all the trouble we've been through,
> What do you think we do?
> We wait!

They start drumming their fingers, which goes into the hand-jive

> As custom dictates,
> We sit and we wait for the pleasure
> Of some Mother's little treasure to ask us to dance.
> Do we feel exploited?

Bridget stands up

> You bet!
> It's like a cattle market,

Sharon stands up

> And yet,

Sue stands up

Rick sheepishly enters the club and apologizes to Eric who allows him back in

> We follow protocol.

Penny notices the boys, who look as though they are about to ask them to dance, and warns the girls who sit down

> As we sit against the wall.
> Faces all aglow,
> We line up in a row.
> Putting on the style,
> We grit our teeth and smile
> And wait.

Gary and Eddie exit to the bar

> And wait.
> And wait.

Rick, embarrassed, hurries after the others into the bar

> We sit and wait.
> We wait.
> We sit and wait.

Gary and Rick enter R. *Eddie enters* C *and they cross to the girls*

Song: Saturday Night Chat

Gary   (*to Penny*) What you doing tomorrow?

Sue is obviously upset by Gary's attention to Penny

	There's a fab movie playing down the ol'Roxy.
Eddie	(*to Bridget*) What you doing tomorrow?
Bridget	Get lost!
Eddie	Well, how d'yer fancy getting lost with me?
Gary	Where you been all my life?
Eddie	Are you on the phone?
Rick	(*to Sharon, pointing to Eddie*) His scooter does a hundred and three.
Sharon	Fancy that.
Boys	Giving 'em the chat, chat, chat. Giving 'em the chat, chat, chat. Giving 'em the yak-itty, yak-itty, yak-itty, yak-itty yak. Yak-itty yak!
Gary	(*to Penny*) Has anybody told you That you look the spitting image of Sandie Shaw?
Eddie	Paul McCartney's my cousin.
Bridget	(*wearily*) Oh yeah?
Gary	Haven't we met somewhere before?
Eddie	Do you fancy a drink?
Gary	Do you live round here?
Rick	(*to Sharon, pointing to Eddie*) His scooter does a hundred and four.
Sharon	Fancy that.

Boys	(*crossing* DL) Giving 'em the chat, (chat) chat, (chat) chat, (chat).
	Giving 'em the chat, (chat) chat, (chat) chat, (chat).
	Giving 'em the yak-itty, yak-itty, yak-itty, yak-itty, yak! yak-itty yak!

Eddie starts gyrating across the floor towards the girls

Sharon	Gawd, who's that coming across the floor?
Bridget	Well, it ain't Mick Jagger and that's for sure.
Penny	He thinks he's cool.
	He thinks he's hip.
Bridget	He's got more spots than me mum's spotted dick.
Girls	(*dancing* DS) Yick-itty, yick-itty, yick-itty, yick-itty yick. Yick-itty yick.

Everyone starts dancing. Gary with Penny. Eddie tries to dance with Bridget. Rick makes eyes at Sharon

Gary	(*to Penny*) Well, don't yer recognise me?
	I'm the fella you've been waiting for all your life.
	So what's your name, then, darling?
Penny	Penny.
Eddie	He asked you for your name, love, not your price.
Gary	Fancy coming outside?
Eddie	(*to Bridget*) You got lovely eyes.
Rick	(*pointing to Eddie*) His scooter does a hundred and five.

Sue in an attempt to make Gary jealous, grabs Rick and starts dancing with him

Sharon	Fancy that.
Eric	Ev'ry Saturday night it's the same.
	They all partake in the chatting-up game.
	He tells her this, she tells him that.
	It all adds up to the Saturday chat.
All	Yack-itty, Yack-itty yack.
Eric	Saturday chat.
All	Yack-itty, yack-itty, yack, yack-itty yack.
	Saturday night, Saturday night, Saturday night chat.
	Saturday night, Saturday night.

The girls return to their seats. Every time Rick tries to talk the others cut in

Gary	Do you live round here?
Eddie	Are you on the phone?
Gary	Been here before?
Eddie	Who's taking you home?
Eric	He tells her this.
	She tells him that.
All	It all adds up to the Saturday chat.

The boys break DL

                    Saturday night, Saturday night chat.

Black-out

From the darkness a toilet is heard flushing

The Lights come up to reveal Eddie and Gary with their backs to the audience, obviously having a pee. Rick is preening himself in the mirror

Rick Who's that bird with Sue, Gary?
Gary Sharon . . . something or other. Just moved in next door to Sue.
Rick Very tasty.
Gary Very tasty indeed, (*shaking himself*) my so-o-n . . .

Gary and Eddie zip up in unison

    . . . If I wasn't so heavily committed I'd be in there meself.
Eddie Sue too much for you is she, Gary?
Gary Do me a favour, Eddie. She don't come into it. I've decided tonight is Big Bertha's lucky night.
Rick (*impressed*) Bertha . . . ? You reckon you can pull her?
Gary She's been sending me signals ever since I got here.
Eddie (*confused*) Signals?
Gary Body Language.

Gary looks in the mirror at Eddie and Rick who are staring blankly

    Desmond Morris.
Eddie Oh, I'm with you. Body language. Yeah. Right of course, Desmond . . .
Gary Morris.
Eddie Right. What about Sue? I thought you two were going together.
Gary Sue . . . ? No, no she's just a stand by in case there ain't nothing tastier in. Anyway, what the eye don't see, son, know what I mean . . . Variety's the spice of life, isn't that right, Rick?
Rick Oh, yeah, absolutely, Gary, absolutely . . . Here, the more the merrier.

The sound of a toilet flushing

Gary Got to spread a little happiness . . . (*He checks himself out in the mirror. Sending Eddie up*) So how about you, Eddie, my man? Got anything lined up?

Eric emerges from the toilet

Eddie Are you kidding? Birds are just naturally attracted to me.
Eric (*as he goes*) Don't you mean flies, Eddie?
Eddie (*following him*) Flies . . . ? No, birds, Eric.

Eddie exits

Gary (*checking himself in the mirror*) I gotta feeling tonight's the night I break my record.
Rick Oh yeah? How many's that, Gary?

Gary Pick a number between five and seven.
Rick (*really impressed*) Six! ... In one night?

Gary smirks superciliously

Gary You?
Rick (*embarrassed*) Me ... Oh, er—fi ...

Gary looks at him

    ... three.
Gary Well, we all gotta start somewhere, Ricky boy. Coming?
Rick Be right with you.
Gary Better get a move on, son. Tonight's your last night remember. You
might not never get another chance ... (*Checking himself in the mirror*)
Brace yourself ladies, Gary is on the prowl.

   Gary growls into the mirror, then exits

*Rick looks in the mirror, very dejected. He gives a pathetic growl in imitation
of Gary*

Rick (*to himself*) Six ... You know what you are? A failure. A complete
failure.

                     Song: Seventeen

                     Seventeen and never done it.
                     Oh, what a waste, oh, what a crime.
                     Seventeen and never done it
                     And I'll soon be past me prime.
                     Ev'ry Saturday night
                     I pray to God tonight's the night
                     That I lose my virginity.
                     But ev'ry Saturday night
                     It's always the same, I'm so ashamed.
                     All of the gang have a bang, but never me.
                     If me mates learnt of my disgrace,
                     I'd never be able to show my face.

Lights pick out Sharon in the girls' loo

Sharon   (*to herself in the mirror*) How I wish I'd never done it.
                     Oh, what a reckless fool I've been.
                     Here I am, a fallen woman
                     And I'm only seventeen.
                     Ev'ry Saturday night
                     I said to myself, no not tonight.
                     No way, no how, oh no siree.
                     Then come that fateful night
                     My iron resolve simply dissolved,
                     When some bloke spiked me Coke
                     With a bottle of Bacardi.
                     If the girls learnt of my disgrace,
                     I'd never be able to show my face.

Lights pick out Eric c

Eric	Don't you find it quite ironic
	Not to say a little mad.
	How the boys boast they have when they haven't,
	And the girls swear they haven't when they have.
Sharon	How I wish I'd never done it.
Rick	I think about it such a lot.
Sharon	What will I say to Mister Right.
Rick	It's no wonder I've got spots.
Sharon	How can I with a clear conscience
	Walk up the aisle dressed in white.
Rick	I'm prepared like all the fellas.
Sharon	Oh, what a fool I've been.
Rick	I've bought me rubber like the rest.
Sharon	And I'm only seventeen.
Rick	And to prevent last minute fumbles
	I put it on before I left.

Sharon |
Rick | *(together)* Seventeen.
Seventeen.
Seventeen.

Lights come up in the Club

Rick joins Eddie and Gary who are chatting to Eric at his desk

Sharon joins Sue and Penny who are sitting chatting to Bridget who is standing with her back to the audience

Eric Animal Magnetism ... ?

Eddie That's right. Yeah. Animal magnetism. Birds can't resist me. I don't know why.

Eric Nor do I, son.

Eddie It's true, Eric. Honest. They're all over me. It's a fight to keep them off.

Eric So how come this irresistible sexual attraction hasn't manifested itself before then?

Eddie Don't ask me. It's just something that's happened. Come on all sudden like ... Strange, innit?

Eric Strange ... ? It's bleeding unbelievable.

Gary Any bird?

Eddie Any.

Eric Okay, so what's the punch line? ... I take it you are joking?

Eddie No.

Gary Oh, leave it out, Eddie ... Coming for a drink, Rick?

They start to leave

Eddie All right, I'll prove it.

They stop

Pick a bird, any bird and I'll have her eating out my hand.

They laugh

I mean it. Go on. Any bird you like.
Gary All right, Eddie ... All right, you're on.

Gary and Rick scan the female members of the audience.

Now she's rather tasty. (*He growls*)
Rick What about her? (*Embarrassed*) Oh, sorry mate.

Gary whispers to Rick. They laugh

Eddie So who's the lucky lady?
Gary (*smugly*) Frigid Bridget.
Eric Ah, that's a bit below the belt, Gary. I mean, give the lad a fighting
chance.
Eddie No, no, Eric, that's right ... Actually, I've always had a bit of a thing
about the ice maiden. In fact ... (*He sings*)

Song: Don't Touch Me!

There ain't nothing that I'd prefer
Than to steam up the windows of Dad's Mini with her.
I dream about it ev'ry night.
Kissing and cuddling and holding her tight.
Oh so tight.
Through the night.
Ev'ry night.

Eric **Gary** (*together*) **Rick**	Eddie, Get her out of your mind. Eddie, You're gonna wind up blind. You're gonna wind up blind. Eddie. Please heed what we say. Eddie. She never gives it away.
Eric	No, no, not that frigid Bridget.
Rick **Gary** (*together*)	No, no, not that frigid Bridget. She'll get you all excited Lead you on then say ...
Eric	No, no, no, no, N-no, n-no, n-no, n-no, no.
Eric **Rick** (*together*) **Gary**	Don't touch me. No, no, no, don't touch me. No, no, no, don't touch me. You can look but you'd better not touch me. You can look but you'd better not touch.

Eddie (*speaking*) We'll see about that. (*Pushing the boys aside*) 'Scusez-moi.

Eddie crosses to Bridget

Wanna dance, Bridget?
Bridget No.
Eric (*imitating Eddie*) Wanna dance, Bridget?

Encouraged by the girls, Bridget reluctantly starts to dance. As Eddie puts his hand on her waist ...

Bridget   (*pushing him away*) Don't touch me.
                               No, no, no.
                               Don't touch me.
                               No, no, no.
                               Don't touch me.
                               You can look but you'd better not touch me.
                               You can dance but you'd better not,

Eddie puts his hand on her waist

                               (*Beating him off*) Oh, no, you'd better not,
                               No, no, you'd better not touch me.
                               You can look but you'd better not touch.

As Bridget turns to walk away ...

(*Speaking. To the girls*) That's told him.
Eddie Here, not so fast, girl ... You fancy me, don't you, Bridget.
Bridget (*flabbergasted*) I beg your pardon ... ?
Eddie It's pointless to deny it. I can read yer signals.
Bridget Signals ... ?
Eddie (*cockily*) Yeah, signals. You know, the old body language ... Desmond ...
Bridget Desmond? Desmond who?

Eddie turns to Gary for help. Gary looks smug

Eddie Y'know that bald git from Zoo Time.
Bridget (*impressed*) Can you really read signals, Eddie?
Eddie Dead right I can, sweetheart.
Bridget (*giving him two's up*) Then read that, you spotty faced little creep.
Eddie (*rubbing his index finger in and out of her "V". Suggestively*) Your place or mine?

Bridget slaps him across the face, turns on her heel and storms off

Sue, Penny and Sharon follow Bridget

Eddie swaggers back to the fellas

(*Smiling broadly*) See that? She can't keep her hands off me.
Eric And you've got the bruises to prove it.

They laugh

Eddie (*indignantly*) What's so funny? She really really fancies me.

They laugh

Eric Give over, Eddie.
Eddie All right, tell you what, I bet by the end of the night she's grabbed me
   whatsit.
Gary Frigid Bridget?

They laugh

Eric You got more chance of winning the Brain of Britain Contest than
   getting her to do that son.
Eddie A quid says you're wrong.
Eric And what we suppose to do then hey, take your word for it?
Eddie No. She'll do it in here, in front of everyone for all to see.
Gary A quid?
Eddie Yeah.
Gary All right, you're on.
Eric Here, not so fast, Gary. (*To Eddie*) We gotta have some ground rules,
   right? I mean, she's got to do it of her own free will and you're not allowed
   to use drugs, bribery or coercion.
Gary Yeah, n'no threats neither.
Eddie Nothing like that.
Eric In that case, Eddie, Eddie my son, you are on.
Rick 'Ere, I think I'll have two bob on that'n'all, Eric.

The Lights fade as Eric pins the money up on the board

*Simultaneously Lights come up in the "Ladies" to reveal Sue and Bridget
looking at themselves in the mirror*

Sue Y'know that Rita.
Bridget The skinny girl?
Sue Skinny ... yeah. She reckons she's going out with Roger Daltrey.
Bridget (*dismissively*) Oh yeah ... ? Last week it was Mick Jagger.
Sue I know ... How lucky can one girl get.

   Shaking her head in disbelief, Bridget exits

*Sue continues to check herself in the mirror. From her expression she obviously
doesn't like what she is seeing. She sings*

Song: Twiggy

   I wish I had a figure like Twiggy's.
   So sylph-like, so incredibly slim.
   My dad says she's lucky
   Her legs don't snap, but he's
   Lying,
   Trying
   To make me feel better.
   I wish I had a figure like Twiggy's,
   Then my life would be one social whirl.
   But gee, am I fed up

Cos with my thirty-eight "D" cup,
I'm just an old-fashioned girl.
If you want to be "in"
You simply have to be slim.
And when they say slim
They mean painfully thin.
Fashion dictates that boobs are a no-no.
The only parts allowed to stick out are
Hip bones, shoulder blades, knee-caps and elbows.

I wish I had a figure like Twiggy's,
Then my life would be one social whirl.
But with my protrusions
I'm under no illusions
I'm just an old fashioned,
Such an old-fashioned,
Just an old-fashioned girl.
Oh yeah, Thanks to Twiggy
I'm just an old-fashioned girl.

Lights go down on the "Ladies" and come up in the Club

During the following dialogue, Eric hovers in the background making increasingly dismissive noises and gestures at each suggestion

Rick ... It's gotta be the Beatles for best group ... They're in a class of their own.
Gary Leave it out. The Stones are much better.
Sue I voted for the Dave Clark Five ... They're absolutely fab.

Gary crosses in front of Sue to Penny

(*Hastily*) Not as fab as you though, Gary.

Gary smirks

Eddie Who's your favourite group, Bridget?
Bridget Sod off.
Eddie What label they on?

Rick laughs

(*To Rick*) Personally, I like the Animals.
Bridget You would.
Gary (*goosing Penny*) Mind you the Kinks 've gotta be in with a chance.
Penny (*running her hand up his leg*) Yeah, and the Searchers.

Unseen by the others, Gary whispers to Penny and they exit to the bar

Rick What about Billy J. Kramer and the Dakotas?
Bridget The Who.
Eddie Billy J. Kramer and the Dakotas.

Bridget gives Eddie a withering look

Sue What about you, Eric? What group do you think's gonna win the *New Musical Express* Poll Winners Contest?
Eric Who do I think?
Sue Yeah.
Eric You really want to know?
Others Yeah.
Eric All right, I'll tell you. (*Singing*)

Song: Cliff

You can
Keep yer Beatles and yer Rolling Stones
Yer Dave Clark Fives and yer Honeycombes.
Yer Animals, yer Kinks, Seekers and yer Searchers,
Billy J. Kramer and his Dakotas.
Cos, after they're all dead and gone
There'll be but one star rockin' on.
Oh, that man with the quiff.
Cliff,
And his four lads.
Cliff Richard and the Shads.

Who could ever forget *D in Love*
And *Summer Holiday* to name just two.

Bridget is talking to Sharon

Oi, Bridget!
There will never be
A better pop song than
Gee Whiz It's You.

So you can
Keep yer Beatles and yer Rolling Stones,
Yer Dave Clark Fives and yer Honeycombes.
Yer Animals, yer Kinks, Seekers an yer Searchers,

(*To Rick*) Old what's his name ...
Rick I know.
Eric ... And his Dakotas
Cos, after they're all dead and gone
There'll be but one star rockin' on.
Oh, that man with the quiff.
Cliff,
And his four lads.
Cliff Richard and the Shads.

(*Speaking*) Who we talkin' about?
Others Cliff.
Eric (*Speaking*) And?
Others And his four lads.

All   Cliff Richard and the Shads.

They all go into a Shadows' routine

                           Cliff Richard and the Shads'.

As they disperse . . .

Bridget (*pointing to the money pinned on the board*) Here, Eric, what's all
   that money doing pinned up there?
Eric That, Bridget, my love, is a monument to man's folly.
Bridget Man's folly . . . ?
Eric You'll never grasp it, dear.
Bridget Oh, wouldn't I . . . ?
Eric (*interrupting*) By the way, what's this I hear about Terry and Shirl?
Bridget (*gloating*) Oh, they've got real problems. Her parents can't stand
   him.
Eric (*incredulously*) Terry . . . ? You'd think anyone'd be proud to have him
   as a future son-in-law, wouldn't you.
Bridget No, no, he's gone really weird . . .

A spotlight picks out Shirl (Penny). *She is kneeling. A large carpet-bag is on
her lap*

Terry (Gary) *enters.*

They look like Sonny and Cher. Terry walks DS

Terry (*to a member of the audience*) Have you told them yet, Shirl?
Shirl Terry . . . Terry, I'm over here.

Terry parts his hair, looks round, and crosses to her

Terry Have you told them yet, Shirl?
Shirl I can't, Terry.

Terry goes down on one knee beside her

Terry It's me isn't it?
Shirl Well . . .

Song: Love On Our Side

Terry	So they don't like my hair.
Shirl	It's not just your hair.
Terry	And the clothes that I wear
Shirl	Nor the clothes that you wear.
Terry	They say I look strange.
Shirl	They say you're deranged.
Terry	Now, that just ain't fair.
Shirl	But I don't care what they say.
	Gonna stay by your side night and day.
	Through thick and thin.
Terry	We'll never give in.

Terry ⎱ *(together)* We will surive.
Shirl ⎰   We got love
                          On our side.

Shirl takes a large poppy from her bag and gives it to Terry who sniffs it. He looks stoned and starts eating it

                 We got love
                 On our side.
                 We ain't ashamed,
                 We got nothing to hide.
                 We wear it with pride.
                 We got love on our side.
                 We got love on our side.
                 We got love on our side.

Shirl   Nothing they say,
                          Nothing they do,
                          Can change my feelings for you.

Terry   When I'm with you
                          I feel strong.
                          Nothing this right
                          Can be wrong.

Terry ⎱ *(together)* Why can't they see you through my eyes?
Shirl ⎰   Maybe then they'd realise
                          There ain't nothing they can do to tear us apart ...
                          Oh, yeah.
                          We got love
                          On our side.
                          We got love
                          On our side.

Terry helps Shirl to her feet

                 We ain't ashamed
                 We got nothing to hide,

Shirl is seen to be very pregnant

                 We wear it with pride.
                 We got love on our side.
                 We got love on our side.
                 We got love on our side.
                 We got love
                 On our
                 Side, Babe.

Terry and Shirl exit

Lights come up in the Club

Sue and Sharon are sitting on the chairs. Eddie and Rick are lounging by the door R

Eric I don't believe it. What—poppies?
Bridget Poppies.

Eric notices Eddie taking a pill

Eric Oi, you ... over 'ere.

As Eddie and Rick cross to Eric, Bridget sits down with the girls

Got a headache or something?

Eric waves Rick away. He moves DL

Eddie Yer what?
Eric I take it they are aspirins you're popping.
Eddie Oh yeah, yeah of course, Eric.
Eric Then how come they're purple? Fruit flavoured are they? How many times have I gotta tell you ... no pills in my club.
Eddie Yeah, yeah, all right.
Eric No it's not all right. Apart from the fact that you could get this place closed, those things'll be the end of you ... You know McCready's after you, don't yer? Says you still owe him for the last lot you had.
Eddie That's where you're wrong, Eric. Everything's cool with ol'Jimmy. He's let me off the hook.
Eric I take it we are talking about the same Jimmy "I'm gonna break that little bleeder's legs if he don't come up with the dosh by Saturday night" McCready?
Eddie Yeah. Some geezer's only gone and wiped the slate for me, hasn't he. Couldn't believe it.
Eric Obviously the big fella upstairs has got a soft spot for dumb animals.
Eddie (*going to leave*) Yeah, right ... (*stopping*) 'Ere, Eric, you had nothing to do with it did yer? Getting me off the hook?
Eric Me? Do you think I'm soft or something? It may have escaped your notice, son, but I run the Club A Go-Go, not the flaming Good Samaritans. My concern for you grotty lot ends the moment you leave these premises.

Gary enters followed shortly after by Penny

Sue and the girls notice them and are suspicious

Eddie I should've known. You only look after number one, right?

Eddie crosses to Rick

Eric Right! You wanna take a leaf out of that book, son. Do you really think I'd dip me hand in me pocket for the likes of you? The man who stays in bed on flag day? Do me a favour. (*To the audience*) Thought the little bleeder had rumbled me.

As Gary crosses to Eddie and Rick, Sue and Bridget start questioning Penny. Sharon moves DR

Gary What was all that about, Eddie?

Music begins under the dialogue

Eddie Nothing, nothing.
Gary Ahhh, have you been taking them pills again?

During the buzz of conversation from the boys and girls, our attention is drawn to Sharon and Rick who are surreptitiously looking at each other

Song: What Do I Do Now?

Sharon	He's looking at me,
	Looking at him,
	Looking at me who's looking at him,
	I wonder what he's thinking.
Rick	She's looking at me,
	Looking at her,
	Looking at me who's looking at her,
	I wonder what she's thinking.
Rick ⎱ *(together)*	What do I do now?
Sharon ⎰	What should my next step be?
	How should I react?
	What should my strategy be?
Rick	Should I move in fast?
Sharon	Should I take it slow?
Rick	Should I act real cool?
Sharon	Or let my feelings show?
Rick ⎱ *(together)*	What do I do now?
Sharon ⎰	What do I do now?
	What do I do now?

Gary and Eddie cross and sit on chairs one and three. After a moment Sue and Penny sit on their respective knees

Sharon	He's smiling at me.
Rick	I'm smiling at her who's smiling at me.
Sharon	I'm smiling at him.
Rick ⎱ *(together)*	I wonder if he/she likes me?
Sharon ⎰	
Rick	She's smiling at me.
Sharon	I'm smiling at him who's smiling at me.
Rick	I'm smiling at her.
Sharon ⎱ *(together)*	I wonder if he/she likes me?
Rick ⎰	What do I do now?
	What do I do now?
	What do I do now?

Rick crosses and stands in the doorway by Eric. Gary and Eddie are obviously getting hot and bothered by the girls who are running their fingers through the boys' hair etc.

Song: What Do You Do?

Gary ⎱ (*to Eric*)   Pssst!
Eddie ⎰

What do you do when a girl sits on your knee
And you start to fantasize?
I ask you, what do you do when you're losing control
And it's more than your temperature that's starting to
rise?
And then she moves out on to the floor
And says . . .

Penny ⎱
Sue   ⎰   Come on, lover, let's dance some more.

Eric   There's one way out of the trap.
                           The jacket flap.

Eric demonstrates the dance

Eddie ⎱   We gotta do the jacket flap.
Gary ⎰   (*To the girls*) Come on, let's do the jacket flap.

Dance routine. After a moment they start dancing close.

(*To Eric*) Psst! Pssst!

What do you do when you're dancing real close
And there's stirrings down below?
Please tell me what do you do when you wanna leave
the floor
Before your growing embarrassment starts to show.
But she holds you, oh so tight,
And says . . .

Penny ⎱
Sue   ⎰   I could dance with you all night

Eric   There's only one way out.
                           You do the crouch.

Eddie ⎱   He's right, we gotta do the crouch.
Gary ⎰   (*To each other*) Let's do that new dance called the
                           crouch.

Eddie and Gary start dancing with each other

Eric No, with the girls!
Rick   But what do you do when you're sitting all alone
                           Feeling happily content?

Sharon smiles at Rick and starts dancing towards him

Then the bird that you fancy suddenly gives you a
smile
And your hipster trousers start resembling a tent.
And then to your dismay
She starts to head your way.

	There's nothing you can do.
	Your embarrassment's on view.
	You wish the floor would open up
	And it would swallow you.
Boys	O-o-o-oh.
Eric	Don't get into a flap.

Eric takes Rick's cap off his head and covers his crutch

Eric |	Just use your cap.
Boys |	And the crouch and the jacket flap.
	The cap and the crouch and the jacket flap.
Eric	So if you're taken by surprise
	Just improvise and
All	Do the cap and the crouch and the jacket flap

As Rick joins in, his cap is left dangling over his crutch

Eric (*indicating the cap*) Rick!

Embarrassed, Rick exits up the stairs

Bridget enters carrying two drinks

Bridget (*handing Penny a drink*) Here, do you know how much these Babychams cost me?
Penny No, how much?
Bridget Three and fourpence.

Rick enters and joins the others

Gary Three and four for two Chamys? That's—er ...
Rick One and eight each.
Gary Yeah, one and eight each.
Sue They were only one and four last Saturday, Bridget.
Bridget I know, that's up fourpence in a week.

Eric wanders over

Gary (*aggressively*) Oh, this is bleeding daylight robbery. I mean, it's getting out of hand. I've a good mind to complain.
Eric About what, Gary?
Gary Oh—er—hello, Eric.
Eric Complain about what?
Gary It's that old barman, Eric. I—er—think he's diddled Bridget. She bought two Chamys, right, and he's charged her three and four.
Eric That's right.
Gary But that's up fourpence since last week.
Eric A necessity. I gotta balance me books, son. Cover me expenses.
Bridget (*to the others*) In other words he's saving up for a new stereo.
Eric I heard that, Bridget. You kids know nothing about business. This place is costing me a bleeding fortune. It's a struggle just to keep me head above water. There are hidden expenses you wouldn't even dream of.

Bridget (*to Sue*) Oh, yeah? Such as?

Song: If You Wanna Have Fun

Eric   The McCready brothers and their protection racket.
                    Every Saturday night I have to hand over a packet.
                    The health inspector and the police want their cut.
                    If I don't cough up then this club'll be shut.
                    Then take the band, well they want a fee.
                    Even go-go Bertha doesn't do it for free.
                    Despite what you think money don't grow on trees.
                    Instead of moaning, how about some sympathy.
                    If you wanna have fun, fun, fun.
                    You gotta pay for it, son, son, son.
                    You can take it from me, me,
                    Nothing in this world comes for free.
                    Who pays for the damages everytime there's a fight?
                    Plus all those glasses broke on a Saturday night?
                    The day one of you put your hand in your pocket
                    I'll drop down dead—so what I say is sod it!

                    If you wanna have fun, fun, fun.
                    You gotta pay for it son, son, son.
                    You can take it from me, me,
                    Nothing in this world comes for free.
                    If you want
All   Fun, fun, fun.
Eric   You gotta pay for it.
All   Fun, fun, fun.
Eric   You know you gotta pay for it.
All   Fun, fun, fun.
Eric   You know you've gotta pay for it, son!
      By the way, it's gonna cost you an extra tanner to get in next week!
All Oh, Eric . . .

Eric exits to the bar

*The others talk amongst themselves, blaming Bridget. Rick stares forlornly at
Sharon*

Rick (*to himself*) Go on, ask her, dammit. Ask her . . . Go on . . . (*He goes to
cross, hesitates, then stops*)

Song: The Long Walk Back

                    I stand transfixed with fear and dread.
                    Should I ask her to dance?
                    Heaven awaits if she says yes,
                    But can I take the chance,
                    Of the long walk back if she says no,
                    Across the empty floor.

The sneering looks, the mocking eyes,
Would cut me to the core.

I've seen so many brave young men
Set out so proud and strong,
Returning bent and shuffling wrecks,
Their nerve and manhood gone.
Oh, God, I humbly beg from you
One minute of your time.
Will her answer be yes or no? Please God, give me a sign.

*There is a flash of lightning and Eddie crosses jauntily to Bridget and asks her
to dance. She refuses. He then asks Sue, Sharon and Penny who also refuse*

Bridget, Sue, Sharon and Penny exit R

Humiliated, Eddie crosses to the mocking Gary

God, you saved me from the long walk back.
From shame and misery.
If not for you that broken lad
Would surely have been me.
Would surely have been me.

Falling to his knees Rick mouths "thank you" to heaven

Black-out

From the darkness hairspray is heard being sprayed in rhythm

*Lights come up to reveal Bridget, Sharon, Penny and Sue in the Ladies,
touching up their make-up and hair. Aerosol cans are used for a rhythm*

Song: Romance/Wham Bam

Sue	My ideal boy would be
	Someone who is faithful, loving and kind.
Bridget	Someone who would always respect me.
Sharon	Someone who would be ...
Others	Someone who would be ...
All (*sighing*)	Romantic'lly inclined.
Bridget	Someone who would buy me choc'lates and flowers
	when they call.
Others	When they call.
Sue	Someone who would walk me to my door
Penny	Expect a kiss and nothing more.
Others	Nothing more.
All	My ideal boy.
	My ideal boy would be
	Someone who is hon'rable and refined.
	Someone who would not take liberties.
	Someone who had more ...
	Someone who had more ...
	Than one thing on their mind.

Lights come up to reveal Gary, Eddie and Rick in the Gents combing their hair etc.

Gary   When it comes to birds, mate.
                  Make no mistake, mate.
                  There's only one thing they want, son.
                  And every fella here's got one.

                  I got one.
                  He's got one.
                  You got one.
Boys   We got one.
                  Wham bam!
                  Wham bam, thank you ma'am
                  That's the only thing they want, man.
                  As often as they can, man.
                  As often as they can.
                  All they want.
Girls   All we want.
Boys   All they want.
Girls   All we want.
Boys   All they want.
Girls   All we want.
Boys   All they want's . . .
Girls   All we want's
                  A little . . .
Boys   Wham bam!
Girls   . . . Romance . . .
Boys   Wham bam, thank you ma'am!
Girls   . . . In our lives.
Boys   Wham bam, thank you ma'am!
Girls   That's all we want . . .
Boys   Wham bam, thank you ma'am!
Girls   From a man.
                  All we want.
Boys   All they want.
Girls   All we want.
Boys   All they want.
Girls   All we want.
Boys   All they want.
Girls   All we want's . . .
Boys   All they want's . . .
Girls   A little . . .
Boys   Wham bam!
Girls   . . . Romance . . .
Boys   Wham bam, thank you ma'am.
Girls   . . . In our lives.
Boys   Wham bam, thank you ma'am
Girls   That's all we want . . .

Boys	Wham bam, thank you, ma'am!
Girls	... From a man.
	All we want.
Boys	All they want.
Girls	All we want.
Boys	All they want.
Girls	All we want.
Boys	All they want.
Girls	All we want.
Boys	All they want.
All	From a man.

Black-out

The Lights come up in the Club

Bridget is standing DS *Eddie is eyeing her from the Club entrance. Eric crosses to the band with one drink*

Eric All right lads, take five (*He hands them the drink*) This one's on the house. (*He crosses* DS. *To the audience*) Snobby little stuck up cow this Bridget, isn't she?

Bridget looks across at him

(*Calling*) All right love?

Bridget crosses and sits down on chair two

Don't know why she bothers coming down here. She never gets off with no-one ... Not like her mother. Rumour has it she's looking for Mister Right. (*Looking round the audience*) Fat chance in this place. (*Noticing Eddie*) Oh, Eddie. Back on the offensive, are we?

Eddie hovers in the background listening to what Bridget is saying

Song: The Boy of My Dreams

Bridget	One day
	I'll meet
	The boy of my dreams.
	Straight out the pages
	Of *True Love* magazine.
	Someone who is sensitive.
Eddie	(*camp*) Hallo, dear.
Bridget	(*rolling her eyes to heaven*) But not as sensitive as that.
	Someone who is strong.
Eddie	(*indicating his biceps*) Feel that, darling.
Bridget	I didn't say a prat.
	One day I'll meet the boy of my dreams.
	One day he'll come,
	My mister right.

Who knows maybe he could be here tonight.
I know he'll be amusing.

Eddie   (*pretending to flash*) Wanna check my meter, Rita?
Bridget   I said amusing, not a git.
So sophisticated.
Eddie   (*breathy*) Ciao, ciao, bambino.
Bridget   (*turning away in disgust*) And his clothes won't smell of
sick.

Eddie gives up and crosses to sit on the steps next to Eric

One day he'll come,
The boy of my dreams.

To him I'll never do wrong,
Never grow old.
I'll always be his princess.
The apple of his eye.
And if I cry
He'll take me on his knee.
And ev'ry morning
He will wake me
With a nice hot ...
Cup of tea.

Can't help
Thinking
I've met him before.
The boy of my dreams
Who I've been waiting for.
He reminds me of someone,
That perfect lad.
Who can it be ...?
(*Shocked*) Oh, my God,
It's my dad.

Perplexed, Bridget exits to the bar R

Eric Not making a lotta headway on the old whatsit front, are we, Edward?
Eddie Double the wager?
Eric You want to throw money at me son, who am I do deprive you of the
pleasure?

Gary enters from the bar

Gary Here, Eddie, got you a half in the bar, mate. All right?
Eddie Cheers, Gary.

Eddie exits to the bar

*Eric pins the money up. He suddenly tenses. Alert. He sniffs the air like a
hound scenting*

Eric (*sniffing*) Oh—oh, I smell trouble. (*Peering around*) It's always the same, every Saturday night ... regular as clock-work. (*Spotting trouble brewing*) Knew it ... (*Pointing*) Over there, look ... It hasn't started yet, but it will.

Song: It Wouldn't Be Saturday Night Without A Fight

Eric   That geezer's smiled at our John's bird.
                'N she's gone and smiled back at the nerd.
                He saunters over to the bar
                Suggestive glances from afar,
                Suggestive glances from afar.

                And unbeknown to her bloke John,
                She gives the lad the old come on.
                Inviting him to make his play,
                A wink's good as a nod they say,
                A wink's good as a nod they say.

                It wouldn't be,
                No, it wouldn't be
                Saturday night
                Without a fight
                It wouldn't be,
                No, it wouldn't be
                It wouldn't be Saturday night,
                Without a fight.

The others enter from the bar R

Throughout the song they concentrate on the fight

Boys   Fight! Fight!
Girls   Saturday night!
Boys   Fight! Fight!
Girls   Saturday night!

Boys   At this point John goes to the loo.
                About the worst thing he could do.
                The lad moves in to take his chance,
                With the classic line, "fancy a dance?"
                With the classic line, "fancy a dance".

                They move across the floor as one.
                His hand slips down and grabs her bum.
                At which point who walks in but John
                And clocks at once what's going on.
Others   He clocks at once what's going on.
Eric   It wouldn't be,
Others   No, it wouldn't be
All   Saturday night
                Without a fight.
                It wouldn't be,

	No, it wouldn't be, It wouldn't be Saturday night Without a fight.
Boys	Fight! Fight!
Girls	Saturday night!
Boys	Fight! Fight!
Girls	Saturday night!
Eric	John calmly crosses to the bloke And grabs the geezer by the throat. The lad starts making with the chat But our John's having none of that.
Others	No, our John's having none of that.
Eric	He belts him once, he belts him twice, In goes the knee, not very nice. Before the fun and games can start I dive straight in and pull them apart.
Others	He dives straight in and pulls them apart.
Eric	And Broderick Crawford's immortal words Follow them through the door. "Leave yer blood in the blood bank "Not on my dance floor!"
	It wouldn't be, No, it wouldn't be Saturday night Without a fight.
All	It wouldn't be, No, it wouldn't be, It wouldn't be Saturday night Without a ...
Eric	Bang, bang, wallop, bang, bang!

Eric leaps off the stage ...

| **All** | Fight! |

Black-out

ACT II

Music (instrumental)

In character, the actors mingle with the audience. After a few minutes Eric enters

Eric (*stopping the band*) Tacet! Tacet! (*To the kids*) All right, you lot, come on, everyone back on the floor. We're gonna do Eric's Hokey-Cokey Shuffle! All right?!

They groan. After being goaded by Eric, they stand around behind him bored

Song: Eric's Hokey-Cokey Shuffle

In! Out!
In! Out!
In! Out! In! Out!
Shake it, shake it all about!

Put yer left foot in.
Put yer left foot out.
In! Out! In! Out!
Shake it, shake it all about.

Put yer right foot in.
Put yer right foot out.
In! Out! In! Out!
Shake it, shake it all about.
Jump to the left.
Jump to the right.
Do the Eric Hokey-Cokey Shuffle on a Saturday night.

Eric notices that no-one is dancing

(*Speaking*) Oi, come on, dance!

The kids drag members of the audience up on stage. Eric gives them a hard time

All   Do the Eric Hokey-Cokey Shuffle.
                 Do the Eric Hokey-Cokey Shuffle.

Eric   Shimmy to the left.
                 Shimmy to the right.
                 Do the Eric Hokey-Cokey Shuffle on a Saturday night.

All	In! Out!
	In! Out!
	In! Out! In! Out!
	Shake it, shake it all about.
Eric	Put yer left hand in.
	Put yer left hand out.
	In! Out! In! Out!
	Shake it, shake it all about.
	Put yer right hand in.
	Put yer right hand out.
	In! Out! In! Out!
	Shake it, shake it all about.
	Twist to the left.
	Twist to the right.
	Do the Eric Hokey-Cokey shuffle on a Saturday Night.
All	Do the Eric Hokey-Cokey shuffle.
	Do the Eric Hokey-Cokey shuffle
	Shimmy to the left.
	Shimmy to the right.
	Do the Eric Hokey,
	Do the Eric Cokey,
	Do the Eric Hokey-Cokey Shuffle on a Saturday ...

Then, as though the record is stuck:

On a Saturday ...
On a Saturday ...
On a Saturday ...
On a Saturday ...
On a Saturday ...

Eric pushes the person next to him. The push is passed around the circle until the member of the audience standing next to Eric bumps into him. The kids react. Eric glares at him

Eric (*speaking*) You're new here, aren't you?

The person replies

Rule one! Don't touch Eric, all right?

The person replies

Good. Don't do it again.
All   Night.
Eric Well, it's ten-thirty and that means?
Others Go-Go time!
Eric Cor-rect! So it's sunglasses on, hands out your pockets and let's go to the bar and give a nice warm Go-Go Club welcome to our resident Go-Go girl . . . "Big Bertha"!

The boys troop out to the bar R followed by Eric

Bridget I don't know that the boys see in her.
Penny You know what the fellas round here are like, they fancy anything in a skirt.

The others agree

Bridget I hear Eric's given her a lovely birthday present.
Sue Oh yeah? What's that?
Bridget Well, what do you give a girl who's got everything?
Penny Dunno ... what?
Bridget Penicillin!

Giggling, Sue and Penny follow Bridget to the bar, Penny dragging a confused Sharon after her

Penny Come on, Sharon, I'll explain it to you.

Cross fade to the alley. Rick is standing outside rehearsing

Rick (*embarrassed*) I fancy you, all right? ... Oh, no. (*In a posh voice*) I just want to tell you, how much I fancy you ... (*Desperately*) Look, I fancy you, all right?

Unnoticed by Rick, Eric enters and stands watching him from the doorway

(*Growing cocky*) I just thought I'd say, darling, how much I fancy you. All right? (*In an American accent*) Hey baby, you wanna know something? I fancy yo-o-u!
Eric What are you doing out here then?
Rick Just getting some fresh air, Eric.
Eric Oh yeah? (*Picking up an empty crate*) Eddie's on a hiding to nothing with that Bridget thing. In an hour's time, he'll be a wiser but poorer man. You're off tomorrow, aren't you?
Rick Yeah.
Eric Well, if I don't see you before you go, look after yourself.
Rick Oh, thanks Eric.
Eric S'alright. (*He goes to exit and stops*) By the way Rick ... I really fancy you too.

Eric exits chuckling at Rick's embarrassment

Sharon enters

Sharon Are you Rick?
Rick Er ... yeah.
Sharon I'm Sharon.
Rick (*awkwardly*) Oh, hi.

There is an embarrassed silence

Sharon Sue says you want to speak to me.
Rick Er ... yeah.

Pause

Sharon Well?

Rick Yeah, right . . . Well . . . You see . . . The thing is . . .

Music intro. Embarassed pause

Sharon Yes?

Rick Um . . . What I wanted to say was . . . is . . .

Music. Embarrassed pause

Sharon (*helpfully*) Yes, Rick . . . ?

Song: I Fancy You

Rick	Did you know that Decca turned the Beatles
	Down in nineteen sixty-one
	And that by nineteen sixty-two
	They'd had a hit with *Love Me Do*?
Sharon	No.
Rick	Oh. I just thought that it might interest you.
	And did you know that Ringo joined the Beatles
	Because Epstein thought the drummer
	That they had, called Peter Best
	Was too good-looking for the rest.
Sharon	No.
Rick	Oh. I just thought that it might interest you.
Sharon	Oh.
Rick	I just thought that I might interest you.

Sharon freezes

Listen to me droning on this way
When all I want to do is say . . .
I fancy you.
Oh, yeah, I fancy you.
Oh, yeah, I fancy you.
So why can't I
Tell you.

Rick goes to kiss Sharon but chickens out at the last moment as she unfreezes

	Did you know the first record the Beatles
	Made was as the backing group
	On *Bring My Bonnie Back To Me*,
	When they were still in Germany?
Sharon	No.
Rick	Oh, I just thought that it might interest you.
Sharon	Oh.
Rick	I just thought that it might interest you.

Sharon freezes

Why do I keep going on this way?
Why can't I bring myself to say . . .

I fancy you.
Oh, yeah, I fancy you.
Oh, yeah, I fancy you.
So why can't I
Tell you.

Sharon unfreezes

Sharon (*bored*) Very interesting ... Was there anything else?
Rick Er ... (*giving up*) No, no ... That's it.

Rick goes to leave

Sharon Before you go back in, Rick, there's something I want to tell you.
Rick (*cringing*) Oh yeah? What's that.
Sharon   I fancy you.
                              I really, do.

They kiss. The sound of a throbbing guitar is heard

Rick What's that noise?
Sharon My heart.

Song: Sentimental Eyes

It started the moment you walked into the Club.
My heart started beating fast.
I knew without doubt I'd fin'lly found the real thing.
I'd found a love I knew would last.

Rick   What set your senses reeling?
                          What is it about me that's so appealing?
Sharon   Oh, your sentimental eyes.
Rick   My what?
Sharon   Your sentimental eyes.
Rick   (*pleased*) I've got ...
Both   Sentimental eyes.
                          Oh, oh, oh, oh.
                          Sentimental eyes.

They kiss

  Bridget enters

Bridget (*to Sharon; bitchily*) I don't mean to interrupt anything Sharon.

Rick and Sharon break away, embarrassed. Bridget goes to speak to Sharon, sees Rick is hanging around and glares at him

  Rick exits

Something absolutely catastrophic's happened.

Bridget whispers in Sharon's ear. She looks shocked

The Lights come up in the Club

Sue enters with Penny

Bridget and Sharon cross to them. Bridget is looking extremely smug

Bridget Hi, Sue.
Sue Hi, Bridget.
Bridget (*to Sharon*) Isn't she taking it well.
Sue (*puzzled*) Taking what well?
Bridget (*insincerely*) Me and my big mouth! (*To Sharon*) She doesn't know.
Sue (*worried*) Know what?
Bridget It's your Gary ... I hate to be the one to tell you, love, but we just saw him with Bertha ... in the alley ... Didn't we, Sharon?
Sharon Well I ... er ... didn't actually ...
Sue They were probably having a chat.
Bridget A chat ... ? With Bang Bang Bertha? The only word she knows, dear, is "yes". You're too easy on him, Sue. You gotta stand up for yourself.

Gary approaches with a drink for himself and Sue

Gary (*to Sue*) How's tricks, love?
Sue (*tearfully*) Oh, Gary ...
Bridget Keep away from her, Gary Williams! (*Comforting Sue*) How could you do it to her?
Gary Do what?
Sue Bang Bang Bertha.
Gary Oh, that!

Gary saunters away

Song: Heartbreaker

Bridget
Penny   (*together*) Stop!
Sharon

During the song Gary eyes-up the girls in the audience

Sue	Heartbreaker,
Gary	(*bored*) Here we go again.
Sue	Breaking my heart in two again.
	Heartbreaker,
	Show some sympathy,
	Don't you know what you're doing to me?
	Heartbreaker stop breaking my heart.
Girls	You know you're tearing her apart.
Sue	Oh-oh.
Girls	Apart
Sue	Oh-oh.
Girls	Apart.
Sue	You're tearing me apart.
Girls	Stop!

Sue	Putting me down.
Girls	Stop!
Sue	Fooling around.
Girls	Stop tearing her apart.
Sue	Stop breaking my heart.
Girls	Stop.
Sue	Before it's too late.
Girls	Stop.
Sue	'N love turns to hate.
Girls	Stop tearing her apart.
Sue	Stop breaking my heart.
	Stop breaking my heart.
Girls	Stop!
Sue	Heartbreaker,
Bridget	This is your last chance.
Sue	Don't turn your back on our romance.
	Heartbreaker,
	Won't you hear my plea?
	You know just how good our love can be.
	Heartbreaker stop breaking my heart.
Girls	You know you're tearing her apart.
Sue	Oh-oh.
Girls	Apart.
Sue	Oh-oh.
Girls	Apart.
Sue	You're tearing me apart.
Girls	Stop.
Sue	Putting me down.
Girls	Stop.
Sue	Fooling around.
Girls	Stop tearing her apart.
Sue	Stop breaking my heart.
Girls	Stop.
Sue	Before it's too late . . .
Girls	Stop.
Sue	'N love turns to hate.
Girls	Stop tearing her apart
Sue	Stop breaking my heart.
	Stop breaking my heart.
Girls	Stop.
	If you don't change and fast
	You'll be the loser.
	You're gonna lose her.
	If you want this love to last
	You gotta stop what you're doing.
	Stop, she ain't fooling.
Sue	I ain't fooling.
Girls	Stop
Sue	Putting me down.

Girls	Stop.
Sue	Fooling around.
Girls	Stop tearing her apart.
Sue	Stop breaking my heart.
Girls	Stop.
Sue	Before it's too late ...
Girls	Stop.
Sue	'N love turns to hate.
Girls	Stop tearing her apart.
Sue	Stop breaking my heart.
Girls	Stop breaking her heart.
Sue	Stop breaking my heart.
Girls	Stop! Breaking her heart. Stop!

Gary Is that an ultimatum?

Sue Well ... er ...

Bridget (*smugly*) It most certainly is.

Sue Er ... yeah.

Gary pours Sue's drink into his beer glass

Gary (*shrugging*) Your loss, darling.

Sue (*devastated*) Bridget ...

Bridget I'll think of something

Bridget exits R *with the girls*

Music

Gary downs his drink

Rick enters R

Rick is ecstatic. As Gary is congratulating him, the lights pick out Eric bopping frantically in front of the band. The boys notice him. He stops in a state of near collapse

Gary (*calling out*) Oi, Eric, you look a little bit knackered.

Eric (*fighting for breath*) No, no ... I'm all right ... I'm fine.

Gary (*to Rick*) Fine ... ? He can hardly stand.

Rick What do you expect, dancing all night at his age. He's gonna do himself a mischief.

Gary (*crossing to Eric. Taking the rise*) He's—er—right, you know, Eric. You wanna knock it on the head. You're getting too old for all this. It's time you stopped bopping.

There is an audible gasp of horror from the band

Eric Stop bopping ... ? Rubber Legs De Vene, remember! I wasn't handed that name on a plate lad! I earned it. (*Pointing to his legs*) These pins, these two stalwarts down here have won no fewer than ...

Gary }
Rick } (*in unison*) Eight.

Eric Nine, "Rock Till You Drop Contests" ... Not local ... nationwide. Nine ... Stop bopping!

Gary I'm sorry . . .
Eric . . . It's what I was born for. My life. My vocation. The only reason
I bought this bleeding club. Stop bopping . . . ! You may as well ask me
to stop breathing . . . Well, I'll tell you something for nothing, lad . . .

Song: Eric's Gonna Keep Doing

                    Eric's gonna keep doing
                    What Eric enjoys doing,
                    Till Eric can't do it no more.
                    And I'm willing to betcha
                    Though they carry me out on a stretcher
                    I'll be doing it at a hundred and four.
                    I've seen the mental torment
                    That packing it in can bring,
                    So I'm gonna make damn sure that I die
                    Shaking my thing.
                    Eric's gonna keep doing
                    What Eric enjoys doing
                    Till Eric can't do it no more.
                    I've boogied with a French girl,
                    Italians and Greeks.
                    Once I get my mojo working
                    There ain't no need for me to speak.

Boys   Eric's gonna keep doing
                    What Eric enjoys doing
                    Till Eric can't do it no more.
Eric   I've boogied in the park.
                    Behind the bus shelter.
                    I'm the lad who's boogied
                    Coming down the helter skelter.
All   Eric's gonna keep doing
                    What Eric enjoys doing
                    Till Eric can't do it no more.

Eric collapses on to the chairs

                    Till Eric can't do it no more.
Boys   Ten minutes've passed and he's fading fast
Eric   (*jumping up*) I've Boogied over breakfast.
                    Boogied walking down the street.
                    I've even been known to boogie
                    Flying at thirty thousand feet.
All   Eric's gonna keep doing
                    What Eric enjoys doing
                    Till Eric can't do it
                    Till Eric can't do it
                    Till Eric can't do it no more
                    Till Eric
                    Can't do it no more.

Gary and Rick collapse on to the chairs

Boys	Do wop bee do bee do bee
	Do wop bee do.
All	Till Eric can't do it no more.

Eric exits to the bar R

Music continues

After a moment Eric returns

Eric	I've boogied on a table.
Boys	Oh, no ...
Eric	Boogied on a two foot shelf.
	If I was as knackered as these two
	I'd have to boogie by myself.
	Eric's gonna keep doing
	What Eric enjoys doing,
	Till Eric can't do it no more.
	Till Eric
	Can't do it no more.
Boys	Do wop bee do bee do bee
	Do wop bee do.
Eric	Till Eric can't do it no more.

Eric exits giving the boys two's-up

Black-out

From the darkness a toilet is heard flushing

Lights come up in the Gents to reveal Eddie who is completely drunk. His every movement is slow and deliberate

Song: Oh, So Bad

Eddie	I feel oh, so bad.
	I feel oh, so yick.
	I feel oh, so, oh no,
	I think I'm gonna be
	Sick.
	Oh, my God, I've
	Never ever felt as bad as this.
	I don't even know my name,
	Where I am, or what day of the week it is.
	(*With sudden realisation*) Hold on a Mo' ...
	There's vomit down me coat.
	I'm standing in the bog
	With me fingers down me throat ...
	It's Saturday night, right?
	It's gotta be Saturday night, right?

Gary enters, the worse for drink

Gary	Oh,
	Oh, no.
Eddie	Gary?
Gary	Eddie?
Eddie	I feel oh, so bad.
Gary	My face has gone all numb.
Eddie	I feel oh, so yuck.
Gary	I want me mum.
Eddie	Oh so . . .
Both	Oh no . . .
Eddie	I think I'm gonna throw . . .
Gary	Up and down the room keeps rolling around.
Eddie	Oh, my God I . . .
Gary	Up and down.
Eddie	. . . Feel so ill, oh I don't want to live.
Gary	The floor keeps spinning it's got a mind of its own.
Eddie	I don't know how I got here . . .
Gary	Round and round . . .
Eddie	Come to that I don't even know where here is.
Gary	Like a record on my gramophone.
Eddie	Hold on a mo, mixed veges on the floor.
Gary	Oh no.
Eddie	Last week's spaghetti hoops congealing on the floor.
	It's the Club A Go-Go.
Gary	I really don't want to know.
Eddie	It's gotta be the Club A Go-Go.
Both	Ev'ry Saturday night it's the same
	Half your money against the wall the other half down the drain.
	At Club A Go-Go.
	On a Saturday night at Club A Go-Go.
	Here we go . . . . . oh . . . . oh . . . oh.
	Take your partners for the . . .
	Stomach churning, bile burning,
	Shoulder shaking, body quacking,
	Oh, no, there she blows,
	Ten-thirty, Saturday night ripple.

They retch five times

Now that's what I call Saturday night.
Eddie You know, I reckon someone spiked my bleeding drink.
Gary What all sixteen pints?

Gary and Eddie exit

The Lights fade and change

Song: Please Don't Tell Me

Rick	Oh please don't tell me That I'm too young to feel the things I'm feeling. That I'm too young to understand love's meaning. It's no more than a passing whim, A spark to flare and quickly dim, That my whole life's ahead of me, There's so much left to do and see ...
Sharon	Don't tell me That what I feel is mere infatuation. It's just some kind of juvenile fixation. I should be out there on the town, That I'm too young to settle down, Well, my friend, I've got news for you It's not a phase I'm going through.
Rick ⎫ **Sharon** ⎭ *(together)*	It's love I'm feeling in my heart, I tell you it's love And I felt it from the start. The moment he/she walked through the door, It was like we'd met somewhere before. I don't know how but one things for sure, I've never ever felt this good, I've never felt this way before.
Sue	So please don't tell me That I'm too young to understand about love.
Gary	That this is someone I will soon grow tired of.
Bridget	That it's a phase I'm going through,
Eddie	Tomorrow I'll find someone new.
Penny	Why can't you try and understand,
All	This isn't just a one night stand.
Boys	It's love
Girls	I'm feeling in my heart.
Boys	I tell you it's love,
Girls	And I felt it from the start.
All	The moment he/she walked through that door, It was like we'd met somewhere before. I don't know how but one thing's for sure, I've never ever felt this good, I've never felt this way before. So please don't tell me
Boys	No, no, no, no, no.
Girls	No, no, no, no, no.
All	That I'm not in love.
Boys	Why do they always put us down. Try and trivialize and minimize and generalize

	And rationalize and criticise our lives.
Girls	Don't they remember what it was like,
	Falling in love on a saturday night,
All	Ev'ry Saturday night.
Boys	It's love
Girls	I'm feeling in my heart.
Boys	I tell you it's love
Girls	And I felt it from the start.
All	The moment he/she walked through that door,
	It was like we'd met somewhere before,
	I don't know how, but one thing's for sure,
	I've never ever felt this good,
	I've never felt this way before.
	So please don't tell me
Boys	No, no, no, no, no.
Girls	No, no, no, no, no.
All	That I'm not in love.
	Please don't tell me,
	I'm not in love.
	Please don't tell me.

The voices fade away

I'm not in love.
I'm not in love.
I'm not in love.
I'm not in love.

The girls are left talking. They are obviously planning something

Gary saunters in from the bar R

The girls sit down

Gary (*cockily; to Sue*) This must be your lucky night, love. I've decided to give you a second chance. Outside and make up.

Gary clicks his fingers and points outside dangling his other hand behind him, expecting Sue to grab it. Sue goes to get up, but Bridget stops her. Half way across Gary realises Sue is not following him

You deaf or something? Come on!

Sue ignores him

Gary holds up his hands and counts off ten on his fingers

Ten, nine, eight, seven, six, five, four, trois, deux ... one. Oh dear, oh dear, oh dear, you've just blown it, love. Your ten seconds are up. (*Crossing to Sharon*) So how about you, darlin'? Fancy a walk on the wild side?

Sue You're pathetic.

Gary looks around to see who she's talking to

You, Gary. You're pathetic. You're so immature.

Song: You're Oh, So . . .

Sue   You've gotta a groovey way of walking,
                           A cool way of talking.
                           You're so hip,
                           So slick,
                           Finger licking good.
                           When girls meet you on the street
                           They think you're so neat.
                           A real gas,
                           So flash,
                           They'd make you theirs if they could.
                           But they don't know you like I know you.
                           They can't see through your disguise.
                           They don't know it's your reflection
                           That you're smiling at when you look them in the eyes.

Sue ⎫ (*together*)   You're oh, so
Girls ⎭   Full of yourself
                           There ain't no room for anything or anyone else.
                           Oh, yes, you're oh, so
                           Full of yourself
                           There ain't no room for anything or anyone else.

Sue   Y'know it really would be something,
                           I mean, really something
                           If you would,
                           You could,
                           Stand inside my shoes.
                           And for that moment we'd change,
                           Some how rearrange,
                           You'd be me,
                           You see,
                           And it follows I'd be you.
Sue ⎫ (*together*)   Cos once you'd seen you like we see you,
Girls ⎭   Maybe then you'd realise
                           That you're not God's gift to women.
                           And as a drag, man, well you really take the prize.
                           You're oh, so
                           Full of yourself
                           There ain't no room for anything or anyone else.
                           Oh, yes, you're oh so
                           Full of yourself
                           There ain't no room for anything or anyone else.

Gary (*imploringly*) But, baby, please . . . I was just having a little joke . . .
Sue   In fact, it's a fact,
                           You ain't even close to where it's at.

Sue, Bridget, Penny and Sharon walk out R

Bridget (*as she goes*) I told you it'd work.

Gary is left stunned

Eric, Eddie and Rick enter from the bar C

Eric (*to Eddie*) Only half an hour to go, Eddie. Still no sign of the Ice Maiden thawing.
Eddie Don't worry. Everything's under control.
Eric Said the Captain of the *Titanic* . . . (*To Gary*) Who stole your *Beano* then? (*Tapping him on the forehead*) Anyone home?
Gary I don't understand it, Eric. It's Sue. She's chucked me. Me! Give me the push.
Eric (*crossing to his desk*) So what's the problem? You're always going on about how you want your freedom.

Eddie joins Eric

Gary Yeah, but that's different. That was before she give me the push . . . It's put a whole new perspective on our relationship. I really fancy her now . . . (*To Rick*) Maybe I should apologize or something. Tell her I'm sorry.
Rick (*embarrassed*) I don't know.
Gary (*crossing to Eric*) What do you think, Eric? Should I apologize to Sue or what?

Eric leads Gary C

Eric (*in a fatherly tone*) Worst thing you could do. A word of advice from one philanderer to another.

Song: Lies

Don't put your faith in truthful explanations.
That's for jerks with no imagination.
Cross your heart and hope to die
And put your faith in that little pork pie.

During the verse, Eric lines up three chairs C

A sullen look of righteous indignation.
Validates the weakest explanation.
Look her squarely in the eye
And put your faith in that old Peckham Rye.

Eric indicates the boys to sit

One thing you've gotta understand,
Happiness and honesty don't walk hand in hand.
So if you want a love-life of harmony,
Follow my philosophy.
Right from the start
You've gotta (*whispering to Gary*)
Gary Lie, Lie. Lie.
Eddie (*to Gary*) Your way out of it.

Rick (*to Gary*)   Lie. Lie. Lie.
Eric   You'll get away with it.
Boys   Lie. Lie. Lie.
Eric   So give it a try.
Gary But I was seen snogging Bang Bang Bertha.
Eric Gary, it is a proven fact that man is born with an inate ability to put
   one over on the fairer sex. Make use of your God-given gifts and . . .
                       Put your faith in falsehood and deception.
                       Cast aside all honest inclinations.
                       Look her squarely in the eye,
                       And put your faith in that little white lie.
   (*Speaking*) So what you gotta do?
Boys   Lie. Lie. Lie.
Eric   Your way out of it.
Boys   Lie. Lie. Lie.
Eric   You'll get away with it.
Boys   Lie. Lie. Lie.
Eric   So give it a try and . . .
Boys   Lie. Lie. Lie.
Eric   You've got the hang of it.
Boys   Lie. Lie. Lie.
Eric   You'll get away with it.
Boys   Lie. Lie. Lie.
Eric   So give it a try . . .
All   And lie
Eric That's my boys.

Black-out

After a moment, the dim outline of the alley can be seen

Sue (*from the darkness*) Oh, Gary, why didn't you tell me Bertha had
   fainted and you were merely giving her mouth to mouth resuscitation?
Gary I didn't think I had to, Sue, I thought you trusted me.
Sue (*tearfully*) I'm so sorry, Gary.
Gary Never mind, you'll know for the next time . . . Give us a kiss.

Sue giggles

Sue Here, Gary . . . What are you doing . . . Gary . . . Stop it . . . Gary!

Song: Baby I Love You

Sue   No!
Gary   Please . . .
Sue   No!
Gary   Please . . .
Sue   No! no! no! no! no! no!
Gary   But, baby, I love you.
Sue   No!
Gary   I really, really, really, really love you.

Sue	No!
Gary	I really, really,
	Really, really, really love you.
	Honest I do.
Sue (*speaking*)	If you loved me, Gary, you'd respect me.
Gary	Baby I respect you.
Sue	No!
Gary	I really, really, really respect you.
Sue	No!
Gary	I really, really,
	Really, really respect you.
	Honest I do.
Sue	No!
Gary	Please ...
Sue	No!
Gary	Please ...
Sue	No! No! No! No! No! No!
Gary	Please ...

From the darkness two other couples join in

Girl 1	No!
Boy 1	Please!
Girl 1	No!
Boy 2	Please.
Girls	No! no! no! no! no! no!

The sound of three slaps are heard

Gary	But, baby, I love you.
Boy 1	Respect you.
Boy 2	Adore you.
Gary	I really, really, really, really need to.
Boy 1	I have to.
Boy 2	I implore you.
Boys	I really, really,
	Really, really, really love you.
	Honest I do ...
Girl 1	No!
Girl 2	No!
Girl 3	No!
Sue	No!
Girls	No! no! no! no! no! no!
Boys	Please ...
Girls	No! no! no! no! no! no!
Boys	Go on ...
Girls	No! no! no! no! no!
	No! no! no! no! no!
	No! no! no! no! no! no!
Boys	But, baby, I love you.

Girls	No! no! no!
Boys	I really, really, really respect you.
Girls	No! no! no!
Boys	I implore you, I adore you ...
Girls	No! no! no!
Boys	Honest I do.
Girls	No!
Boys	Please.
Girls	No!
Boys	Please.
Sue	No! no! no! no! no! no!

Pause

(*Speaking*) We-e-ll, if you promise not to tell.
Gary Honest. I promise.
Sue All right.

Pause

Gary (*in a stifled whimper*) Oh, my God ...

Pause

Sue Well, come on, Gary. (*Pause*) Gary?
Gary It's no good, Sue ... I've -er- got a headache.
Sue (*tearfully*) Oh, Gary ...

Lights come up in the alley. Gary is alone looking totally dejected

Song: P.E.

Gary

I've tried thinking of cricket,
Boxing and school.
Tennis, soccer, snooker and darts.
I've tried them all.
I've tried thinking of so many things
That my poor brain hurts.
But nothing,
No nothing,
No nothing seems to work.

You meet a girl at the dance.
She says she fancies you,
You know this is your big chance.
You dance real close
Show her everything you've got.
The way she's dancing
You know she's getting hot.
You take her outside,
She coyly says all right.
Oh, boy, at last.
This could be your night.

Your brain is telling you
"Slow, man, slow".
Oh-oh, oh-oh,
Oh-oh, oh-oh, oh-no-oo-oo-oo.

Premature ejaculation.
It's the curse of the younger generation.
Nothing can compare
To the humiliation of
Premature, oh!
Premature, no!
Premature ejaculation.

Band   One more time ...
Gary (*speaking*) Too late!
Oh, no.

The alley reverts to the Club. Sue is sitting on the chair being comforted by Bridget and Penny. Rick and Sharon are sitting on the edge of the stage DR. Eddie is leaning in the doorway to the bar R. Gary stands L staring sadly at Sue

Eric (*indicating Gary*) One problem after another isn't it.

Song: Who'd Be Seventeen?

Sexual awakening with all its taboos.
Horrendous stories you heard in the loos.
It's small wonder that they're all so confused.
I ask you, who'd be seventeen.

Eric notices Eddie taking a pill

Giving Eric a dismissive look, Eddie exits to the bar

Wet behind the ears, straight out of school.
Can't tell 'em nothing, can you, they know it all.
I just stand back and wait for them to fall.
I ask you, who
Who'd be seventeen?

Oh, seventeen
When your life was all extremes.
Up or down, but no in-betweens.
Oh no, oh no.

Gary crosses to Sue. They make up

Oh, seventeen
When your life was still filled with dreams.
Instead of with just might have beens.
Oh no, oh no.
Not when you're seventeen.

Remember how everything you did was brand new?
Well, not to anyone else, but it was to you.
It seemed there was nothing you couldn't do.
I ask you, who
Who'd be seventeen.

Eric crosses to his stool

Who'd be seventeen.
Who'd be seventeen.
Who'd be seventeen.

Eddie enters carrying his coat over his arm, which he holds in front of him

Eric Come to admit defeat, Edward, my son?
Eddie I may have lost the odd battle, but the war is not yet over. (*He takes a pound note out of his pocket*) I'm wearing her down.
Eric (*taking it from him*) I know the feeling.

As Eric pins the notes up on the board, Sharon, obviously upset, moves DC. *Rick stands looking at her*

Eddie (*indicating Rick and Sharon*) What's up with Sonny and Cher then?
Eric I think Rick must've just told her he's leaving tomorrow.
Eddie Oh, right.
Eric (*crossing to the band*) All right lads, let's wrap it up, it's nearly midnight. Last number. Make it a real smoochy. Pass me maracas. A—one, two, three and . . .

Rick and Sharon start dancing cheek to cheek. Sharon is very upset. Eddie, keeping his lap covered by the coat, sits next to Penny. Giving him a withering look, Bridget drags Penny away. They move R

Song: Last Saturday Night

Rick   Turn the music and the lights down low.
                           Hold me like you'll never let me go.
                           This is our
                           Last Saturday night.
Sharon   Come tomorrow don't know where you'll be.
                           All I'll have left are my memories.
                           Of our last,
                           Last Saturday night.

Rick ⎫ (*together*)   I wanna remember you as you are this night.
Sharon ⎭   The look of love shining in your eyes.
                           And though we have to say goodbye
                           My love for you will never die.
                           I'll remember our last Saturday
                                 night.

Sharon breaks away

Music under dialogue

(*Speaking. Tearfully*) Do you have to go, Rick?
Rick You know I do, love.
Sharon It seems I've no sooner found you than I've lost you.
Rick I'll be back.
Sharon You'll find someone else.
Rick Never . . . While I'm away I'll write home every day and I'll send all
my loving to you.
Sharon Oh, Rick.

Rick	(*together*)	Although we have to say goodbye.
Sharon		My love for you will never die.
		I'll remember our last Saturday night.
		Last Saturday night.
		Last Saturday night.

Eddie shuffles his chair C

Eric See what I mean? Everything's a drama when you're seventeen. He's
only going to Butlin's for a week with his mum.

Eddie speaks to Eric

Oi, Bridget, Eddie wants a word with you.
Bridget (*coldly*) Well I don't want a word with him, thank you very much!
Eric Come on, move yourself. I want to lock up.

With a sigh of resignation, Bridget crosses to Eddie. The rest gather around

Bridget (*coldly*) What is it?
Eddie (*ingratiating*) I just want to say I should never have made those lewd
suggestions to a girl like you. It was in bad taste. So in front of everyone,
I'd like to say I'm very, very sorry . . .
Bridget (*turning to leave; haughtily*) Well, it's too late for that!
Eddie . . . and by way of an apology I've bought you a present. (*He throws
off his coat to reveal a gift-box on his lap*)

Eric takes one look, groans and crosses to get the money

Bridget (*stopping*) A present . . . (*She turns back*) Really? . . . (*Smiling to the
girls*) Ooo, I love surprises.
Eddie (*smirking*) You'll love this then.
Bridget What is it?
Eddie Guess. It's something you've always wanted.
Bridget An E-type Jag?
Eddie No.
Bridget (*to herself*) Something I've always wanted . . . (*To the girls*) My
mind's a total blank. (*To Eddie*) I give up.
Eddie (*a sudden idea*) I tell you what, close your eyes, have a feel and see if
you can guess what it is.

The boys realise what is going to happen. Everyone eggs her on

Bridget Oh, all right.
Eddie No peeping. Promise?

Bridget Promise.

Bridget closes her eyes and holds out her hand. With a smug look Eddie holds his hand out. Eric goes to place the money into it

Eric (*to Eddie*) This is worth every penny, Edward, my son ... yours I believe, Bridget.

Eric grabs the box off Eddie's lap and thrusts it at Bridget. Her hand goes straight through. There is no bottom. Bridget's expression changes from one of bewilderment to total anger as she realises what Eddie was planning. She screams and lashes out knocking Eddie off his chair

Strobe lighting

All hell breaks loose. It is like an early Beatles' film

As the set reverts to the prologue, Eric passes in front counting the money

Song: Slice Of Saturday Night/Club A Go-Go (*reprise*)

All	I've had me a slice of Saturday night.
	I've had me a slice of Saturday night.
	I've had me a slice of Saturday night, tonight, tonight.
	I've had me a slice of Saturday night.
	Saturday night.
	I've had me, had me a slice
	Of Saturday night.
	Saturday night.
	Saturday night.
	Saturday night.
Eric	So I'll say good-night to one and all.
Others	All.
Eric	From one of life's great finishing schools.
Others	Schools.
Eric	This breeding ground of the teenage dream.
Others	Dream.
Eric	This microcosm of the teenage scene.
Others	Scene.
Eric	Where the music's loud and the lights are low,
	Where the kids learnt all they had to know.
	Goodnight to you all from the Club A Go ...
All	Go.
	Saturday night.
	Saturday night.
	Saturday night.
Girls	Met some fellas.
All	Saturday night.
Boys	Grabbed us some chicks.
All	Saturday night.
Girls	Dug the music.

All	Saturday night.
Boys	Drunk till we're sick
All	Saturday night.
Boys	Blown all our money.
All	Saturday night.
Girls	Heard all the chat.
All	Saturday night.
	Had a good time,
	Man, cos that's where it's at.
	We're so cool.
	Real trendy.
	So fab.
	So ... yeah, yeah, yeah! yeah!
	I've had me a slice of Saturday night
	I've had me a slice of Saturday night.
	I've had me a slice of Saturday night, tonight, tonight.
	I've had me a slice of Saturday night.
	Saturday night.
	I've had me, had me a slice of
	Saturday night.

Black-out

PROPERTY LIST

Only essential properties, as mentioned in the text, are listed here. Further dressing may be added at the director's discretion

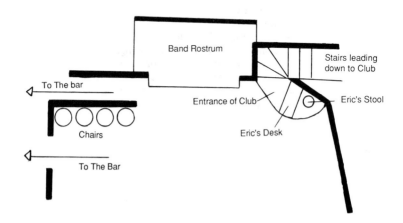

ACT I

Off stage: Various glasses of drink

Personal: **All girls:** handbags containing money, make-up, combs, hairsprays, etc.
Eddie: overcoat, money
Shirl: carpet bag. *In it:* poppy
Rick: cap
Eric: cash box, money, rubber stamp, glass

ACT II

Off stage: Crate (for alley)

Personal: **Eddie:** pills, gift box

LIGHTING PLOT

Composite set. An underground Club incorporating other settings

Prologue

To open: Lights pick out cast members

Cue 1	**Cast** reach up to turn off lights *Black-out*	(Page 2)

ACT I

To open: Lights pick out Eric

Cue 2	**Eric** (singing): "... Club A Go-Go" *Lights come up on the Club*	(Page 3)
Cue 3	**Girls** (singing): "... Disappear in the loo." *Crossfade to the Ladies*	(Page 5)
Cue 4	**Girls** (singing): "We burst onto the scene." *Lights revert to Club*	(Page 5)
Cue 5	**All** (singing): "... Saturday night chat." *Black-out*	(Page 8)
Cue 6	Toilet flushes *Lights up on Gents*	(Page 8)
Cue 7	**Rick** (singing): "... able to show my face." *Lights up on Ladies*	(Page 9)
Cue 8	**Sharon** (singing): "... able to show my face." *Lights up on Eric*	(Page 9)
Cue 9	At end of song *Seventeen* *Fade Lights in toilets. Lights up on Club*	(Page 10)
Cue 10	**Eric** pins money on board *Fade Lights in Club. Lights up in Ladies*	(Page 13)
Cue 11	At end of Song *Twiggy* *Lights down on Ladies, up on Club*	(Page 14)
Cue 12	**Bridget:** "... he's gone really weird." *Spotlight on Shirl*	(Page 16)
Cue 13	**Terry and Shirl** exit *Lights up on Club*	(Page 17)
Cue 14	**Rick** (singing): "Please God give me a sign." *Flash of lightning*	(Page 23)

Cue 15	**Rick** falls to his knees *Black-out*	(Page 23)
Cue 16	Hairspray sprayed *Lights up on Ladies*	(Page 23)
Cue 17	**All** (singing): "Than one thing on their mind." *Lights up on Gents*	(Page 23)
Cue 18	At end of song *Romance/Wham Bam* *Black-out. Lights up on Club*	(Page 25)
Cue 19	At end of song *It Wouldn't be Saturday Night Without A Fight* *Black-out*	(Page 28)

ACT II

To open: Lights up on Club

Cue 20	**Penny:** "I'll explain it to you." *Crossfade to alley*	(Page 31)
Cue 21	**Bridget** whispers in Sharon's ear *Lights up on Club*	(Page 33)
Cue 22	**Gary** congratulates Rick *Lights pick out Eric bopping*	(Page 36)
Cue 23	**Eric** gives the boys two's-up *Black-out*	(Page 38)
Cue 24	Toilet flushes *Lights up on Eddie in the Gents*	(Page 38)
Cue 25	**Gary and Eddie** exit *Lights fade and change*	(Page 39)
Cue 26	**Eric:** "That's my boys." *Black-out. Pause. Faint light up on alley*	(Page 44)
Cue 27	**Sue:** "Oh, Gary ..." *Lights up on alley*	(Page 46)
Cue 28	At end of song *P.E.* *Alley Lights revert to Club*	(Page 47)
Cue 29	**Bridget** knocks Eddie off his chair *Strobe lighting*	(Page 50)
Cue 30	When ready *Revert to Prologue lighting*	(Page 50)
Cue 31	At end of song *A Slice of Saturday Night/Club A Go-Go* *Black-out*	(Page 51)

EFFECTS PLOT

ACT I

Cue 1   In black-out   (Page 8)
           Toilet flushes

Cue 2   **Rick:** ". . . more the merrier."   (Page 8)
           Toilet flushes

Cue 3   **Rick:** ". . . give me a sign."   (Page 23)
           Crash of thunder

ACT II

Cue 4   **Eric** gives two's-up. Black-out   (Page 38)
           Toilet flushes

MADE AND PRINTED IN GREAT BRITAIN BY
LATIMER TREND & COMPANY LTD PLYMOUTH
MADE IN ENGLAND